WHEN DESTINY CALLS THE MAN THE MOMENT DEMANDS WORKBOOK

A Call to Courageous Leadership in Uncertain Times

By

Peace Philip

Copyright © 2025

All rights reserved. No part of this publication may be reproduced, distributed, or transmitted in any form or by any means, including photocopying, recording, or other electronic or mechanical methods, without the prior written permission of the publisher, except in the case of brief quotations embodied in critical reviews and certain other noncommercial uses permitted by copyright law.

Disclaimer

This book is intended for informational and educational purposes only. The author and publisher assume no responsibility for errors or omissions or any outcomes resulting from the use of this material. Readers are encouraged to seek professional advice where applicable.

Chapter 1: Recognizing the Moment 9

Section 1: Understanding the Call 9

    The Essence of "The Moment" 10

    Pivotal Moments as Catalysts for Change 10

    Embracing the Uncertainty 11

    The Inner Dialogue of a Leader 12

Section 2: Self-Awareness and Reflection 12

    Discovering Personal Strengths 13

    Confronting Weaknesses and Vulnerabilities 13

    Engaging in Structured Reflection 14

    The Role of Emotional Intelligence 15

    Readiness for Change 15

Section 3: Identifying Opportunities 16

    The Art of Perception 16

    Developing a Proactive Mindset 17

    Practical Tools for Opportunity Identification 17

    Turning Insight into Action 18

    Cultivating a Growth-Oriented Environment 19

    Integrating Lessons Learned 19

Conclusion 20

Chapter 2: Building Core Character 22

    Section 1: Defining Your Values 22

        Understanding the Role of Values in Leadership 22

Identifying Your Core Values 23

The Intersection of Values and Ethics 23

Exercises for Defining Your Values 24

The Impact of Clearly Defined Values on Leadership 24

Section 2: Cultivating Integrity and Authenticity 25

The Essence of Integrity in Leadership 25

Strategies for Cultivating Integrity 25

Authenticity: Being True to Yourself 26

Exercises for Enhancing Integrity and Authenticity 26

Overcoming Challenges to Integrity and Authenticity 27

The Transformative Power of Integrity and Authenticity 28

Section 3: Developing Resilience 28

The Importance of Resilience in Leadership 28

Cultivating Mental Toughness 29

    Strategies for Building Mental Toughness 29

Exercises to Enhance Resilience 30

Learning from Failure 30

Building a Support Network 31

Developing Emotional Resilience 32

    Techniques for Enhancing Emotional Resilience 32

Integrating Resilience into Daily Leadership 32

The Long-Term Benefits of Resilience 33

Conclusion 34

Chapter 3: Crafting Vision and Strategy 35

Section 1: Creating a Personal Mission 36

Understanding the Essence of a Personal Mission 36

Aligning Your Mission with Your Values and Purpose 37

Steps to Crafting Your Personal Mission 37

Exercises to Develop Your Mission 38

The Transformative Impact of a Personal Mission 39

Section 2: Strategic Goal Setting 39

The Importance of Setting Measurable Goals 39

Translating Vision into Actionable Goals 40

Steps to Effective Goal Setting 40

Tools and Frameworks for Goal Setting 41

Overcoming Barriers in Goal Setting 42

Exercises for Strategic Goal Setting 42

The Role of Adaptability in Goal Setting 43

Section 3: Planning for Impact 43

Connecting Daily Actions to Long-Term Objectives 43

Developing an Impact-Oriented Mindset 44

Methods to Align Daily Actions with Strategic Goals 44

Creating a Strategic Impact Plan 45

Overcoming Common Challenges in Planning for Impact 46

    Integrating Impact Planning into Your Leadership Style 47

    The Lasting Benefits of a Well-Executed Impact Plan 48

  Conclusion 48

Chapter 4: Leading with Influence 51

  Section 1: Mastering Communication 51

    The Role of Communication in Leadership 52

    Strategies for Enhancing Communication Skills 53

    Exercises to Master Communication 54

    Overcoming Communication Barriers 55

    The Impact of Mastering Communication 56

  Section 2: Inspiring Others 56

    The Art of Inspiration 57

    Techniques for Motivating Teams 58

    Exercises for Inspiring Others 59

    The Transformative Power of Inspiration 60

  Section 3: Navigating Conflict 60

    Understanding the Nature of Conflict 61

    Strategies for Effective Conflict Resolution 61

    Practical Tools for Navigating Conflict 62

    Handling Common Conflict Scenarios 63

    Maintaining Harmony While Driving Progress 64

    Exercises for Conflict Navigation 65

    The Long-Term Benefits of Navigating Conflict Effectively 66

  Conclusion 66

Chapter 5: Sustaining Legacy and Growth 68

  Section 1: Embracing Continuous Learning 69

    The Imperative of Lifelong Learning 69

    Strategies for Continuous Learning 69

    Exercises and Practices for Continuous Learning 71

    The Role of Curiosity and Humility 72

    Learning from Failure and Success 72

    The Benefits of a Continuous Learning Mindset 72

  Section 2: Maintaining Long-Term Focus 73

    The Challenge of Long-Term Vision in a Fast-Paced World 73

    Strategies for Long-Term Focus 73

    Overcoming Short-Term Distractions 75

    Aligning Actions with Vision 75

    The Importance of Resilience and Adaptability 76

    Exercises for Sustaining Long-Term Focus 76

    The Long-Term Rewards 77

  Section 3: Crafting Your Legacy 77

    Defining Legacy in Leadership 77

    Steps to Crafting a Meaningful Legacy 78

    Strategies for Building a Leadership Brand 79

Overcoming Challenges in Legacy Building 80

Exercises for Crafting Your Legacy 80

The Emotional and Psychological Aspects of Legacy 81

The Enduring Benefits of a Well-Crafted Legacy 81

Integrating Legacy with Daily Leadership Practices 82

Conclusion 83

Chapter 1: Recognizing the Moment

In every life, there comes an instant—a juncture where events, decisions, and opportunities converge in a way that has the power to change the course of one's destiny. This chapter is devoted to understanding and embracing those pivotal moments that demand a decisive response, laying the groundwork for transformative leadership. It is an invitation to step into awareness, assess one's inner landscape, and ultimately, to transform challenges into opportunities for growth and impact.

Section 1: Understanding the Call

At the heart of leadership lies an acute sensitivity to the call of the moment. "The moment" is not simply an arbitrary point in time; it is a dynamic interplay of circumstance, readiness, and the inherent potential for change. Recognizing this call requires both an internal attunement and a willingness to engage with the unexpected, to see beyond routine challenges and to grasp the hidden opportunities that lie within them.

The Essence of "The Moment"

Every significant achievement or breakthrough in history has been catalyzed by moments when individuals chose to step forward despite uncertainty. These instances are characterized by a sense of urgency—a deep internal knowing that the present holds the key to future transformation. The call of the moment is often subtle; it might appear as a whisper amidst the clamor of everyday life, urging you to seize an opportunity that many might overlook. In these times, the difference between ordinary action and extraordinary leadership is defined by one's ability to listen to that inner voice.

Consider moments of historical import: leaders in times of crisis, innovators who redefined industries, and everyday heroes whose quiet courage brought about profound change. In each case, there was a moment when the call was clear—a call that demanded courage, commitment, and vision. For many, this call is experienced as a spark that ignites a transformation in mindset. It is the realization that the status quo is not enough and that there exists a possibility for something far greater.

Pivotal Moments as Catalysts for Change

Pivotal moments often serve as inflection points in our lives. They compel us to reexamine our beliefs, challenge our limitations, and redefine our purpose. When we learn to see these moments for what they truly are—a bridge between who we are and who we can become—we open ourselves up to transformative experiences.

Every setback can be reinterpreted as a setup for a comeback, and every challenge can be transformed into an opportunity for growth.

This transformative process is rooted in the belief that we are not defined solely by our past actions or current circumstances, but by our potential to evolve. Recognizing the call of the moment requires a willingness to confront the unknown and to trust that every experience—no matter how challenging—carries within it the seeds of future success. When leaders act with conviction during these times, they not only change their own lives but also inspire others to embrace their potential for transformation.

Embracing the Uncertainty

Understanding the call also means embracing uncertainty. Often, the most transformative moments are accompanied by ambiguity. The path ahead is not clearly mapped out, and the stakes are high. Yet, it is precisely in this uncertainty that true leadership is forged. By accepting that the future is never entirely predictable, you can free yourself from the paralyzing fear of failure and instead focus on the possibility of growth and renewal.

Engaging with uncertainty involves a deliberate shift in perspective—from seeing risk as a barrier to viewing it as a necessary ingredient for innovation and progress. Leaders who are willing to venture into the unknown understand that every decision, even if it leads to temporary discomfort or setbacks, contributes to a larger narrative of growth and resilience. They recognize that the call of the moment is not just about responding to external pressures, but also about internal evolution—a process that refines character and expands one's capacity for greatness.

The Inner Dialogue of a Leader

The call of the moment often begins as an internal dialogue—a quiet conversation with oneself that questions complacency and demands accountability. This internal conversation challenges you to reflect on your values, assess your aspirations, and align your actions with your deepest beliefs. It is a process of self-inquiry that not only sharpens your awareness but also emboldens you to take risks and pursue opportunities that might otherwise seem out of reach.

Developing this inner dialogue requires regular reflection and mindfulness. It means pausing amidst the rush of daily life to ask yourself: "What is the moment asking of me?" By cultivating this habit of introspection, you begin to recognize patterns in your behavior and identify the conditions that inspire you to act. Ultimately, this awareness is the first step in transforming everyday experiences into defining moments of leadership.

Section 2: Self-Awareness and Reflection

To truly recognize and respond to the call of the moment, it is essential to cultivate a deep understanding of oneself. Self-awareness is the cornerstone of personal development and leadership. By engaging in thoughtful reflection and honest self-assessment, you build the foundation needed to navigate change with clarity and confidence.

Discovering Personal Strengths

Self-awareness begins with a recognition of your inherent strengths. These are the qualities that have carried you through previous challenges and will serve as assets in times of uncertainty. Take time to reflect on your past achievements—both big and small—and identify the skills, attitudes, and behaviors that enabled your success. Perhaps it was your ability to remain calm under pressure, your knack for innovative problem-solving, or your talent for rallying others around a common goal. These strengths are not merely traits; they are powerful tools that can be harnessed to meet new challenges head-on.

To deepen this understanding, consider engaging in activities that prompt self-reflection. Journaling, meditation, and feedback from trusted peers can provide valuable insights into the unique attributes you bring to every situation. Ask yourself questions like: "What have I excelled at in the past?" "Which qualities do others admire in me?" "How have my strengths contributed to my successes?" Through such reflective practices, you not only validate your capabilities but also gain a clearer picture of the areas where you can build further resilience.

Confronting Weaknesses and Vulnerabilities

While it is important to celebrate your strengths, true self-awareness also involves an honest examination of your weaknesses and vulnerabilities. Leaders who are effective in the long run understand that acknowledging areas for improvement is not a sign of weakness but rather a commitment to continuous growth. Reflect on situations where you may have fallen short or encountered challenges that seemed insurmountable. What lessons did these experiences teach you? How can you address these gaps in your skill set or mindset moving forward?

This process of confronting weaknesses can be challenging. It may involve uncomfortable truths about your habits, fears, or limitations. However, by embracing these aspects of yourself with compassion and openness, you pave the way for transformative change. Recognize that every leader has areas that need nurturing, and that personal development is an ongoing journey. Use your vulnerabilities as a guide to seek out new strategies, training, or mentorship that can bolster your capabilities and prepare you for the call of the moment.

Engaging in Structured Reflection

Reflection is most powerful when it is structured and deliberate. Consider setting aside regular intervals—daily, weekly, or monthly—for in-depth self-assessment. During these sessions, ask yourself targeted questions about your recent experiences, emotional responses, and decision-making processes. For instance:

- What moments in the past week challenged my assumptions or pushed me out of my comfort zone?
- How did I respond to uncertainty, and what could I have done differently?
- In what ways did I rely on my strengths, and where did I notice gaps in my performance?

These reflective exercises not only deepen your understanding of your personal journey but also help you recognize patterns that may either propel or hinder your progress. Documenting your insights in a dedicated journal can serve as a roadmap, highlighting your evolution as a leader and helping you track the progress of your growth over time.

The Role of Emotional Intelligence

A key component of self-awareness is emotional intelligence—the ability to recognize, understand, and manage your emotions, as well as those of others. Emotional intelligence empowers you to navigate the complexities of interpersonal relationships and to respond to the call of the moment with empathy and insight. By developing a heightened sense of emotional awareness, you can better discern the emotional undercurrents in challenging situations and adjust your responses accordingly.

Practice techniques such as mindfulness meditation, active listening, and empathetic engagement with peers. These practices not only enhance your emotional regulation but also deepen your capacity for connection and collaboration. In moments of uncertainty, emotional intelligence becomes a critical asset, enabling you to balance logic with compassion, and to inspire trust and confidence in those around you.

Readiness for Change

Ultimately, self-awareness is about preparing yourself for change. Recognizing your personal strengths, acknowledging your weaknesses, and engaging in structured reflection are all steps toward a state of readiness—a readiness to step into the unknown and to harness the energy of the moment. This preparedness is what transforms potential into action, ensuring that when the call of the moment arrives, you are equipped not just to respond, but to lead with clarity and conviction.

Section 3: Identifying Opportunities

The final piece of recognizing the moment lies in the ability to identify opportunities where others might see only obstacles. This skill is essential for transforming challenges into catalysts for growth and for harnessing the energy of pivotal moments to drive lasting change.

The Art of Perception

Opportunities often present themselves in disguise, masked as routine problems or even as crises. Developing a keen eye for opportunity means learning to view obstacles from multiple perspectives. Instead of immediately focusing on the difficulties, train yourself to ask: "What can I learn from this situation?" and "How might this challenge reveal a new path forward?" By reframing problems as opportunities for innovation and improvement, you open yourself to creative solutions that can lead to breakthrough success.

This shift in perspective is not always intuitive—it requires deliberate practice and mental agility. One effective method is to engage in brainstorming sessions where every challenge is dissected and analyzed for its hidden potential. Invite colleagues, friends, or mentors to participate in these discussions, as collective wisdom often reveals insights that individual reflection might miss. Over time, you will find that your ability to spot the silver lining in even the most daunting scenarios improves, turning obstacles into stepping stones for growth.

Developing a Proactive Mindset

Leaders who consistently transform challenges into opportunities possess a proactive mindset. This mindset is characterized by a willingness to take initiative, to experiment with new ideas, and to embrace change rather than shy away from it. It involves anticipating potential roadblocks and preparing contingency plans, thereby ensuring that you remain agile in the face of uncertainty.

To cultivate this proactive approach, consider setting personal challenges that push you out of your comfort zone. For example, volunteer for projects that seem daunting or unfamiliar. These experiences force you to confront uncertainty head-on, gradually building your capacity to see opportunity where others might see risk. Additionally, surround yourself with individuals who embody this proactive spirit—mentors and peers who inspire you to take bold action and who offer constructive feedback when needed.

Practical Tools for Opportunity Identification

There are several practical tools and frameworks that can help you sharpen your ability to identify opportunities:

- **SWOT Analysis:** Evaluate your personal or professional situation by identifying Strengths, Weaknesses, Opportunities, and Threats. This structured approach not only highlights areas for improvement but also pinpoints specific opportunities for growth.
- **Mind Mapping:** Create visual diagrams that connect different ideas, challenges, and potential solutions. This creative process can reveal

unexpected relationships and opportunities that might not be immediately obvious.

- **Scenario Planning:** Imagine various future scenarios based on current trends or challenges. By visualizing multiple outcomes, you can better prepare for different eventualities and identify opportunities that align with your long-term goals.

Using these tools consistently will help you develop a systematic approach to opportunity identification. Over time, you will become adept at recognizing the subtle signals that indicate when a challenge is, in fact, an invitation to innovate, lead, and make a lasting impact.

Turning Insight into Action

Identifying an opportunity is only the first step; the true test lies in the ability to act on it. When you perceive a challenge as a gateway to innovation, the next step is to develop a plan of action. This involves setting clear objectives, identifying the resources needed, and outlining the steps required to transform a challenge into a concrete outcome.

Action plans should be flexible and adaptive, recognizing that the path to success is rarely linear. Embrace the idea of iterative progress—taking small, deliberate steps that collectively lead to significant change. Maintain a balance between planning and execution, ensuring that you remain responsive to feedback and new information as the situation evolves.

Cultivating a Growth-Oriented Environment

While personal readiness is essential, the environment in which you operate plays a crucial role in opportunity recognition. Surround yourself with a culture that encourages experimentation, rewards creative problem-solving, and supports calculated risk-taking. Whether in a corporate setting, a community organization, or your personal network, fostering a growth-oriented environment can amplify your ability to spot and seize opportunities.

Leaders can influence their surroundings by modeling curiosity and resilience. Share your successes and failures openly, creating a safe space for dialogue and innovation. By nurturing an atmosphere where everyone is empowered to contribute ideas and challenge the status quo, you not only enhance your own leadership capabilities but also build a collective momentum that propels the entire group forward.

Integrating Lessons Learned

Each moment of challenge provides valuable lessons that, when integrated, refine your ability to identify opportunities in the future. Reflect on past experiences—both those that resulted in success and those that fell short of your expectations. Analyze what factors contributed to the outcomes, and consider how you might apply these insights in future scenarios.

By systematically documenting your experiences and the lessons learned from them, you create a personal repository of knowledge that serves as a guide during uncertain times. This ongoing process of learning and adaptation is critical to long-term success, ensuring that every challenge is viewed not as a setback but as a stepping stone to greater leadership and influence.

Conclusion

Recognizing the moment is a multifaceted journey that begins with understanding the call of the moment, deepens through self-awareness and reflection, and culminates in the identification of opportunities where others see only obstacles. Each section of this chapter has been designed to empower you with the mindset and tools necessary to transform uncertainty into a powerful catalyst for leadership.

As you move forward, keep in mind that the call of the moment is not a single event but a recurring invitation to grow, innovate, and lead. Embrace it with courage, be honest with yourself through reflection, and always be on the lookout for opportunities hidden within challenges. In doing so, you will not only fulfill the demands of the present but also lay the foundation for a future defined by transformative leadership and enduring impact.

By integrating these insights and practices into your daily life, you are taking the first crucial step on a journey that promises not only personal fulfillment but also the potential to inspire and uplift those around you. Every moment holds the possibility of greatness—recognize it, act on it, and become the leader the moment demands.

This chapter sets the stage for a transformative journey by urging you to listen to the call of the moment, cultivate self-awareness, and harness the potential of every challenge. As you engage with these principles, remember that leadership is not defined by the absence of obstacles but by the capacity to turn those obstacles into opportunities for lasting change.

Chapter 2: Building Core Character

Building core character is the foundation of exceptional leadership. It is the internal compass that guides every decision, the moral fiber that shapes how we relate to others, and the resilience that helps us navigate adversity. In this chapter, we delve deep into the essential elements of character—defining your values, cultivating integrity and authenticity, and developing resilience. Over the next 3000 words, we will explore these three critical components through thoughtful analysis, real-life examples, and practical exercises to help you forge a robust and enduring character that supports effective leadership.

Section 1: Defining Your Values

Understanding the Role of Values in Leadership

At the core of every great leader is a set of values that defines who they are and how they interact with the world. Values are the principles and beliefs that guide behavior and decision-making. They serve as an internal benchmark against which actions are measured and provide a consistent framework for evaluating choices, even when external pressures mount.

When you define your values, you are essentially charting a moral map. This map helps you navigate complex ethical dilemmas and ensures that your leadership is both principled and purposeful. Leaders who operate from clearly defined values not only inspire trust but also create environments where those around them feel secure, respected, and aligned with a common purpose.

Identifying Your Core Values

Identifying your core values is a reflective process that requires deep introspection. Start by asking yourself questions such as:

- What qualities do I admire in others?
- What principles do I refuse to compromise on?
- Which moments in my life have defined who I am today?

Write down a list of qualities and principles that resonate with you. These might include honesty, compassion, courage, fairness, accountability, or innovation. Once you have a list, look for patterns or themes that recur. For instance, if you find that you consistently value honesty and transparency, you may consider these your foundational values.

It is also helpful to reflect on key moments in your personal or professional life when you felt most fulfilled. What were the underlying principles that contributed to those feelings? Often, the emotions tied to these memories can reveal the values that matter most to you.

The Intersection of Values and Ethics

Your values form the basis of your ethical framework. Ethics are the standards that govern behavior in a community or organization, and personal ethics are the expression of your inner values in everyday actions. For leaders, having a clear ethical stance is essential because it creates consistency in decision-making and helps in building a reputation of reliability and trustworthiness.

Consider the case of a leader who values fairness above all. When faced with a decision that might favor one group over another, such a leader is likely to opt for a solution that ensures equitable treatment for all. This ethical commitment not only upholds their values but also reinforces the trust that others place in them. In today's fast-paced and often morally ambiguous world, leaders who stand by their values, even in difficult times, become beacons of integrity.

Exercises for Defining Your Values

1. **Value Journaling:** Dedicate time each day or week to writing about moments when you felt proud or disappointed by your actions. Analyze these instances to identify recurring themes that hint at your core values.
2. **Role Model Reflection:** Identify people you admire—be they public figures, mentors, or historical leaders—and list the values you believe drive their behavior. Compare these with your own and consider what aspects resonate with you.
3. **Prioritization Matrix:** Once you have a list of values, rank them in order of importance. This exercise forces you to confront situations where values might conflict and decide which principles are non-negotiable.

The Impact of Clearly Defined Values on Leadership

When your values are clear, your leadership becomes more authentic and focused. Decision-making becomes less about reacting to circumstances and more about deliberate, principled action. A leader who understands and lives by their values can navigate crises with confidence, knowing that their actions reflect their deepest beliefs.

Moreover, sharing your values openly with your team or community fosters an environment of transparency and trust. People are more likely to follow a leader who is clear about what they stand for because it provides them with a sense of security and direction. In turn, this shared understanding of values can drive collective purpose and commitment.

Section 2: Cultivating Integrity and Authenticity

The Essence of Integrity in Leadership

Integrity is often described as the alignment between words and actions. It is the quality of being honest, ethical, and consistent in all aspects of life. For a leader, integrity is not just a personal virtue; it is the bedrock upon which trust and respect are built. When leaders demonstrate integrity, they inspire loyalty and create a culture where ethical behavior is the norm.

Integrity means making decisions that are not only legally sound but also morally right. It is about standing by your principles even when it is inconvenient or unpopular. This commitment to ethical behavior often distinguishes true leaders from those who simply hold positions of power.

Strategies for Cultivating Integrity

1. **Accountability Practices:** One effective way to cultivate integrity is to establish systems of accountability. This might involve regular self-assessments, seeking feedback from peers, or setting up mentorship relationships where you can openly discuss your challenges and decisions.

2. **Transparency in Decision-Making:** Share your decision-making process with those around you. By explaining how your choices are guided by your values, you demonstrate that your actions are rooted in a clear ethical framework. Transparency not only builds trust but also invites constructive dialogue.
3. **Commitment to Consistency:** Consistency in behavior reinforces the perception of integrity. When you act in ways that are true to your stated values, regardless of the situation, you establish a reputation for reliability and ethical steadfastness.

Authenticity: Being True to Yourself

Authenticity is closely related to integrity but focuses more on the internal alignment of your beliefs, actions, and presentation. Being authentic means embracing your true self, with all its strengths and imperfections, and expressing that self in your leadership role. Authentic leaders are not afraid to show vulnerability, admit mistakes, or reveal the human side of their journey.

Authenticity creates a powerful connection between a leader and their followers. When people see that you are genuine and relatable, they are more likely to trust you and invest in your vision. Authenticity also empowers you to stand up for your beliefs, even in the face of opposition, because you are not trying to conform to external expectations or norms.

Exercises for Enhancing Integrity and Authenticity

1. **Reflective Storytelling:** Write about times when you had to make a difficult decision that tested your values. Reflect on how you handled the situation

and what you learned from it. Sharing these stories can help reinforce your commitment to integrity.

2. **Feedback Loops:** Regularly seek honest feedback from trusted colleagues or mentors about your actions and decisions. Use this input to identify areas where you might be straying from your core values or where you can be more authentic.

3. **Mindfulness Practices:** Engage in mindfulness or meditation exercises that help you become more aware of your thoughts, emotions, and impulses. Increased self-awareness is a crucial step toward ensuring that your actions align with your true self.

Overcoming Challenges to Integrity and Authenticity

In a world where external pressures and rapid change can lead to compromise, maintaining integrity and authenticity is a constant challenge. Leaders often face situations where the right choice may not be the easiest or most popular. It is in these moments that your commitment to your values is truly tested.

One common challenge is the temptation to sacrifice ethical principles for short-term gains. For instance, a leader might be tempted to overlook minor ethical breaches in order to achieve a larger objective. However, this can create a slippery slope where compromising on values becomes normalized. The key is to remain vigilant and consistently remind yourself of the long-term benefits of unwavering integrity.

Another challenge is the pressure to conform. In highly competitive environments, there may be a strong incentive to mimic the behavior of others, even if it means deviating from your own principles. Cultivating a strong sense of self and a clear understanding of your values can help you resist these pressures. Remember that true leadership is not about following the crowd but about setting a course that is guided by your internal compass.

The Transformative Power of Integrity and Authenticity

When you lead with integrity and authenticity, you create an environment where trust flourishes. This trust is not only essential for effective team dynamics but also for building a legacy of ethical leadership. Integrity inspires confidence among colleagues, partners, and stakeholders, while authenticity fosters deep, genuine connections.

The benefits of these qualities extend beyond the workplace. In personal relationships and community engagements, integrity and authenticity are the cornerstones of respect and mutual understanding. Leaders who embody these qualities become role models, encouraging others to prioritize ethical behavior and genuine self-expression.

Section 3: Developing Resilience

The Importance of Resilience in Leadership

Resilience is the capacity to bounce back from setbacks, adapt to change, and keep moving forward despite challenges. In leadership, resilience is not merely a desirable trait—it is essential. The journey of leadership is fraught with obstacles, disappointments, and failures. What distinguishes successful leaders is not the absence of adversity but the ability to recover and learn from these experiences.

Resilience involves mental toughness, emotional strength, and the capacity to maintain a positive outlook even when faced with seemingly insurmountable difficulties. It is the force that drives leaders to persevere, innovate, and ultimately, succeed.

Cultivating Mental Toughness

Mental toughness is the ability to stay focused, motivated, and effective in the face of challenges. It is built over time through deliberate practice and the development of strategies that reinforce a resilient mindset.

Strategies for Building Mental Toughness

1. **Embrace a Growth Mindset:** View challenges as opportunities for learning and development rather than as threats to your success. A growth mindset allows you to see setbacks as temporary obstacles that can be overcome with effort and perseverance.
2. **Set Realistic Goals:** Break larger challenges into smaller, manageable tasks. Achieving these incremental goals builds confidence and reinforces your ability to handle adversity.
3. **Practice Positive Self-Talk:** Replace negative, self-defeating thoughts with positive affirmations. Remind yourself of past successes and your inherent ability to overcome obstacles.
4. **Establish Routines:** Create daily habits that promote mental clarity and focus. Whether through exercise, meditation, or structured planning, consistent routines can strengthen your mental fortitude.

Exercises to Enhance Resilience

Developing resilience is a practical process that involves a variety of exercises and strategies. Consider incorporating the following into your routine:

1. **Resilience Journaling:** Keep a dedicated journal where you document challenges you face, how you responded, and what you learned from the experience. Over time, this record becomes a testament to your ability to grow through adversity.
2. **Stress-Management Techniques:** Practice techniques such as deep breathing, progressive muscle relaxation, or mindfulness meditation. These methods can help you manage stress and maintain composure under pressure.
3. **Scenario Analysis:** Regularly engage in exercises that simulate potential challenges you might face in your leadership role. Consider different scenarios and plan how you would respond. This proactive approach not only prepares you for actual adversity but also builds confidence in your ability to navigate uncertainty.
4. **Physical Conditioning:** Physical well-being is closely linked to mental resilience. Engage in regular physical activity, as exercise has been shown to reduce stress and improve mood, thereby enhancing your overall resilience.

Learning from Failure

Failure is an inevitable part of any leadership journey, but it is also one of the greatest teachers. Embracing failure as a learning opportunity is key to building resilience. Each setback provides valuable insights that can inform future decisions and strategies. Rather than allowing failure to define you, use it as a stepping stone to success.

Reflect on past failures and identify the lessons learned. Ask yourself:

- What factors contributed to this setback?
- What could I have done differently?
- How can I apply these insights moving forward?

By reframing failure as a necessary component of growth, you can reduce the fear associated with taking risks. This perspective not only builds resilience but also fosters a culture of innovation and continuous improvement.

Building a Support Network

Resilience is not built in isolation. Surrounding yourself with a supportive network of mentors, peers, and trusted advisors is critical. These individuals can provide guidance, encouragement, and constructive feedback when you face challenging situations.

Engage in regular discussions with your support network to share experiences, brainstorm solutions, and reflect on your progress. The collective wisdom of a diverse group can offer fresh perspectives and bolster your capacity to overcome adversity. Remember that even the strongest leaders benefit from the insights and support of others.

Developing Emotional Resilience

Emotional resilience is the ability to manage and recover from emotional setbacks. It involves recognizing your emotions, understanding their impact on your behavior, and developing strategies to maintain a balanced state of mind.

Techniques for Enhancing Emotional Resilience

1. **Mindfulness Meditation:** Regular mindfulness practices help you remain present and aware of your emotional state. This increased awareness enables you to regulate your responses to stress more effectively.
2. **Emotional Expression:** Don't be afraid to express your feelings in a constructive manner. Whether through conversation, creative expression, or physical activity, allowing yourself to process emotions can prevent them from building up into overwhelming stress.
3. **Cognitive Restructuring:** Challenge negative thought patterns by reframing them in a more positive light. Instead of viewing a setback as a personal failure, consider it a challenge that can be overcome with effort and perseverance.
4. **Empathy for Self:** Practice self-compassion. Recognize that everyone faces difficulties, and treat yourself with the same kindness and understanding you would offer a friend in a similar situation.

Integrating Resilience into Daily Leadership

To truly develop resilience, it must become part of your daily leadership practice. This involves not only responding to challenges as they arise but also anticipating potential obstacles and preparing for them in advance. Consider integrating resilience training into your regular leadership routines. This could mean setting aside time each week to review your challenges, celebrate your successes, and plan for future obstacles.

Create a personal resilience plan that includes:

- **Goals for Growth:** Define specific objectives related to your resilience, such as improving your stress-management techniques or expanding your support network.
- **Actionable Steps:** Outline the daily or weekly practices you will implement to build your mental and emotional toughness.
- **Measurement and Reflection:** Establish metrics for evaluating your progress. Regularly review your experiences and adjust your plan as needed.

The Long-Term Benefits of Resilience

Resilience is not only about surviving adversity; it is about thriving in spite of it. Leaders who develop strong resilience are better equipped to handle the inevitable ups and downs of their professional and personal lives. They are more innovative, more adaptive, and more capable of turning challenges into opportunities for growth.

Over time, the process of building resilience transforms your approach to leadership. It shifts your perspective from one of caution and fear to one of confidence and possibility. By embracing resilience as a core aspect of your character, you position yourself not only to lead effectively in the present but also to inspire those around you to cultivate their own inner strength.

Conclusion

Building core character is a continuous journey—a process of defining your values, cultivating integrity and authenticity, and developing the resilience necessary to overcome life's inevitable challenges. In this chapter, we have explored how your values form the ethical foundation of your leadership, how integrity and authenticity reinforce trust and connection, and how resilience empowers you to transform setbacks into stepping stones for success.

By defining your values, you establish a clear moral framework that guides every decision and action. By cultivating integrity and authenticity, you ensure that your leadership is not only principled but also genuine, forging deeper bonds with those you lead. And by developing resilience, you equip yourself with the mental and emotional fortitude needed to navigate the uncertainties of leadership with confidence and grace.

As you move forward, remember that character is not a static trait—it is forged over time through reflection, action, and the willingness to learn from every experience. Embrace each opportunity for growth as a chance to build a stronger, more resilient, and more authentic version of yourself.

In your journey toward effective leadership, the work you do on your character will pay dividends in every aspect of your life. You will find that decisions become clearer, challenges more surmountable, and relationships more meaningful. Ultimately, the core character you build today will be the guiding light that not only leads you through difficult times but also inspires those around you to strive for greatness.

As you integrate the practices outlined in this chapter into your daily routine, take the time to reflect on your progress. Celebrate your achievements, learn from your setbacks, and continuously refine your approach. In doing so, you will create a legacy of leadership that is grounded in strong values, unwavering integrity, and resilient determination—a legacy that will stand the test of time.

Let this chapter be a reminder that the journey to effective leadership is as much about internal development as it is about external achievement. Build your core character with intention, and you will become the kind of leader who not only meets the challenges of today but also inspires a brighter future for all.

By embracing the practices and insights shared in this chapter, you are taking a decisive step toward developing a leadership style that is both principled and powerful. Building core character is a lifelong commitment, and as you continue on this journey, you will discover that the strength of your values, the authenticity of your actions, and the resilience of your spirit are the true measures of your leadership potential.

Chapter 3: Crafting Vision and Strategy

Developing a clear vision and a strategic plan is essential for any leader who aims to make a lasting impact. This chapter will guide you through creating a personal mission that aligns with your values, setting strategic and measurable goals, and planning for impact by connecting your daily actions with long-term objectives. By the end of this chapter, you will have a comprehensive roadmap to transform your vision into tangible results.

In today's rapidly changing world, leaders need more than just good intentions—they require a solid strategy to drive meaningful progress. Whether you're leading a team, an organization, or your own personal journey, crafting a vision that is both inspiring and actionable is the cornerstone of effective leadership. This chapter is divided into three sections that build upon each other, ensuring that every aspect of your strategic framework is covered.

Section 1: Creating a Personal Mission

Understanding the Essence of a Personal Mission

A personal mission is a concise statement that reflects who you are, what you stand for, and what you hope to achieve. It is the north star that guides your decisions, energizes your actions, and keeps you focused on what truly matters. Unlike vague aspirations, a well-articulated mission is actionable and measurable, serving as the foundation for all your future endeavors.

Your mission should align with your core values and long-term purpose. It provides clarity during challenging times, reinforcing the reasons behind your choices and the path you've chosen. A strong personal mission not only motivates you but also inspires those around you. Leaders with clear missions are seen as dependable, focused, and committed to making a difference.

Aligning Your Mission with Your Values and Purpose

The first step in creating your personal mission is reflection. Ask yourself the following questions:

- **Who am I at my core?** Consider your strengths, passions, and the qualities that define you.
- **What do I truly value?** Reflect on the principles that guide your behavior—integrity, compassion, innovation, or excellence.
- **What is my purpose?** Think about the legacy you want to leave and the impact you wish to have on the people and communities around you.

Once you have reflected on these questions, begin to craft your mission statement. For example, if you value innovation and community empowerment, your mission might be: "To leverage innovative solutions to empower communities, drive positive change, and create sustainable opportunities for growth." This statement is clear, action-oriented, and directly tied to core values and a broader purpose.

Steps to Crafting Your Personal Mission

1. **Brainstorming:**

Dedicate time to free writing about your dreams, values, and the impact you wish to create. Allow your thoughts to flow without censorship. Consider moments in your life when you felt most alive, most purposeful, or most connected to your values. Note the common themes that emerge.

2. **Drafting Your Statement:**

Synthesize the insights from your brainstorming session into a draft mission statement. Aim for clarity and conciseness. A strong mission statement should be memorable and easy to communicate to others. Keep it specific enough to guide your actions yet broad enough to allow for growth and evolution.

3. Refining Through Feedback:

Share your draft with trusted friends, mentors, or colleagues who understand your aspirations. Their feedback can help you refine your language and ensure that your mission resonates both with you and with those who might join your journey.

4. Testing and Iteration:

Your mission is a living document. Test its validity by aligning it with your daily actions and decisions. Revisit and refine it regularly as you gain new insights or as your circumstances evolve. This iterative process ensures that your mission remains relevant and inspiring.

Exercises to Develop Your Mission

- **Vision Journaling:** Spend a few minutes each day reflecting on your experiences and how they align with your values. Document insights that could influence your mission statement.
- **Mind Mapping:** Create a visual representation of your core values, passions, and long-term goals. Use this map as a guide to see how they interconnect, forming the basis of your mission.
- **Legacy Reflection:** Write a letter to your future self or to someone you admire, describing the impact you hope to have. This exercise helps

crystallize what is most important to you and can be distilled into your personal mission.

The Transformative Impact of a Personal Mission

A clear personal mission brings purpose and direction. It serves as a benchmark for decision-making, ensuring that every step you take is aligned with your ultimate goals. In times of uncertainty or stress, returning to your mission can provide reassurance and clarity, reminding you why you chose your path in the first place.

Leaders with well-defined missions are more resilient. They view setbacks as temporary detours rather than dead ends because they understand that their mission transcends any single challenge. By keeping your mission at the forefront of your mind, you ensure that your actions contribute to a larger, more impactful vision of success.

Section 2: Strategic Goal Setting

The Importance of Setting Measurable Goals

A vision, however inspiring, requires actionable steps to materialize. Strategic goal setting bridges the gap between your mission and your daily actions. Goals transform abstract ideas into concrete, measurable targets. They provide direction and benchmarks for success, making it easier to track progress and adjust your strategy as needed.

Goals should be Specific, Measurable, Achievable, Relevant, and Time-bound (SMART). This framework ensures that your goals are realistic yet challenging, and that they can be quantified so that you know when you've achieved them.

Translating Vision into Actionable Goals

When setting goals, start by breaking down your vision into manageable components. Think about what needs to happen for your mission to be realized and identify the key milestones along the way. For instance, if your mission is to empower communities through innovation, your goals might include launching a pilot project, securing partnerships with local organizations, and measuring the impact of your initiatives.

Steps to Effective Goal Setting

1. Identify Key Areas:

Consider the major components of your mission. These could be professional growth, community engagement, innovation, or personal development. Break these areas down into specific objectives.

2. Establish Clear Metrics:

Determine how you will measure success. Define key performance indicators (KPIs) or other metrics that align with each goal. For instance, if your goal is to build a network of community partners, set a target number for new partnerships and a timeline for achieving them.

3. Set Realistic Deadlines:

Time-bound goals create a sense of urgency and help prioritize actions. Assign realistic deadlines that challenge you without setting you up for failure.

4. Create a Roadmap:

Develop a detailed plan that outlines the steps needed to achieve each goal. Identify the resources required, potential obstacles, and strategies to overcome them. A well-structured roadmap provides clarity and keeps you accountable.

5. Regular Review and Adaptation:

Strategic goals should be dynamic. Set regular intervals to review progress and adjust your strategy as necessary. This flexibility allows you to respond to changes in your environment and stay aligned with your overall mission.

Tools and Frameworks for Goal Setting

Several practical tools can aid in strategic goal setting:

- **SMART Goals Framework:**

Use the SMART criteria to ensure that every goal is well-defined. For example, instead of saying "I want to increase community engagement," specify "I will increase community engagement by 20% over the next six months by launching three new initiatives."

- **OKRs (Objectives and Key Results):**

This method helps you define what you want to achieve (objectives) and how you will measure progress (key results). OKRs create alignment between daily actions and overarching strategic objectives.

- **Gantt Charts and Timelines:**

Visual representations of your goals and deadlines can help you see the big picture and track your progress over time. These tools are particularly useful for complex projects with multiple interdependent tasks.

Overcoming Barriers in Goal Setting

While setting goals is essential, it can also be challenging. Common barriers include:

- **Lack of Clarity:** Unclear goals lead to confusion and diluted efforts. Make sure each goal is articulated with precision.
- **Overwhelm:** Trying to achieve too much at once can be paralyzing. Prioritize your goals and tackle them incrementally.
- **Resistance to Change:** Sometimes, the habits and routines that once served you can become obstacles. Embrace new strategies and be willing to adapt.
- **Fear of Failure:** The possibility of not meeting a goal can be intimidating. Frame setbacks as learning opportunities rather than failures, and adjust your plans accordingly.

Exercises for Strategic Goal Setting

- **Goal Mapping:** Write down your long-term vision and then create a detailed map of the goals needed to achieve it. Break each goal into smaller tasks and assign deadlines.
- **Visualization:** Imagine what success looks like in each area of your mission. Visualize the milestones and the impact they will have, reinforcing your commitment to the goals.

- **Peer Accountability:** Share your goals with a mentor or trusted peer who can offer feedback and hold you accountable. Regular check-ins can provide valuable support and motivation.

The Role of Adaptability in Goal Setting

The environment in which you operate is constantly evolving. A key component of strategic goal setting is the willingness to adapt your goals in response to new information or changing circumstances. This flexibility is not a sign of weakness; it is a hallmark of resilient and effective leadership. Regularly reassess your goals, celebrate your progress, and adjust your strategies to ensure that you remain on track. Adaptability ensures that your goals continue to align with both your personal mission and the broader trends affecting your industry or community.

Section 3: Planning for Impact

Connecting Daily Actions to Long-Term Objectives

Planning for impact means ensuring that every action you take moves you closer to your long-term vision. It involves creating a consistent, deliberate strategy where daily routines, decisions, and initiatives contribute to an overarching plan. Impact is not an accidental by-product of success—it is the intentional result of aligning every effort with your mission and goals.

When you plan for impact, you view each day as an opportunity to build momentum. Even the smallest actions can have a cumulative effect, leading to significant outcomes over time. This section will explore methods to ensure that your daily habits are in sync with your long-term objectives, creating a virtuous cycle of continuous improvement and growth.

Developing an Impact-Oriented Mindset

An impact-oriented mindset requires a commitment to excellence in every detail of your work. It's about recognizing that your actions, no matter how small, contribute to the bigger picture. This perspective shifts your focus from short-term gains to long-term sustainability and influence. It encourages you to ask:

- How does this task align with my core mission?
- What is the long-term benefit of this action?
- How can I ensure that my efforts are both efficient and effective?

Cultivating this mindset involves regular reflection and accountability. By setting aside time each day to review your actions and assess their impact, you can continuously fine-tune your approach and maintain a clear focus on your ultimate objectives.

Methods to Align Daily Actions with Strategic Goals

   1. Daily Planning and Prioritization:

Start your day by reviewing your long-term goals and mission. Identify three key actions that will make the most significant contribution toward these objectives. Use planners, digital tools, or even simple to-do lists to organize your tasks according to their strategic importance.

   2. Time Blocking:

Allocate specific blocks of time to focus on activities that directly contribute to your mission. Protect this time from interruptions to ensure that you remain dedicated to high-impact work. Time blocking not only improves productivity but also reinforces the connection between daily activities and long-term goals.

3. **Reflective Practices:**

At the end of each day, reflect on the tasks completed and assess how they align with your strategic vision. Consider what worked well and what could be improved. Journaling or brief meditation sessions can help consolidate insights and inform future planning.

4. **Leveraging Technology:**

Use productivity and project management tools to keep track of your progress. Digital calendars, task management apps, and performance dashboards can provide real-time insights into your achievements and help you identify areas for adjustment.

5. **Continuous Learning and Adaptation:**

Embrace a cycle of continuous learning by seeking feedback, attending workshops, or reading relevant literature. Incorporate new strategies and techniques into your daily routine, ensuring that your approach remains innovative and effective.

Creating a Strategic Impact Plan

To ensure that every day contributes to your long-term vision, it's essential to develop a strategic impact plan. This plan should outline how daily actions, short-term projects, and larger initiatives interconnect. Consider the following components when creating your plan:

- **Mission Alignment:** Clearly articulate how each key action or project contributes to your overall mission. This alignment provides clarity and motivation.
- **Milestone Mapping:** Break your long-term goals into quarterly or monthly milestones. Define what success looks like at each stage and track your progress accordingly.
- **Resource Allocation:** Identify the resources—time, money, personnel, or technology—you need to execute your plan. Ensure that your resources are distributed in a way that maximizes impact.
- **Feedback Loops:** Establish mechanisms for receiving regular feedback on your progress. Whether through team meetings, performance reviews, or personal reflection sessions, use this feedback to adjust your plan as needed.
- **Celebrating Small Wins:** Recognize and celebrate the achievement of milestones along the way. Celebrations not only build momentum but also reinforce the link between daily effort and long-term impact.

Overcoming Common Challenges in Planning for Impact

Even the best-laid plans can encounter obstacles. Common challenges include:

- **Distractions and Procrastination:** Maintaining focus in a world filled with distractions requires discipline. Use techniques like the Pomodoro Technique, eliminate unnecessary interruptions, and hold yourself accountable through structured schedules.

- **Changing Priorities:** As circumstances evolve, so might your priorities. Ensure that your strategic plan remains flexible enough to accommodate necessary adjustments without losing sight of your mission.
- **Burnout:** Overcommitting without balancing work and rest can lead to burnout. Build in regular breaks, delegate when possible, and practice self-care to sustain long-term impact.
- **Measurement Difficulties:** Sometimes, the impact of daily actions is hard to measure. Develop clear, quantifiable metrics for your projects, and review them regularly to ensure that you are on track.

Integrating Impact Planning into Your Leadership Style

The most impactful leaders are those who consistently align their daily actions with their overarching strategic vision. To integrate impact planning into your leadership style, consider these approaches:

- **Modeling Consistency:** Lead by example. Show your team how every task, no matter how small, contributes to a larger goal. This modeling inspires others to adopt an impact-oriented mindset.
- **Encouraging Team Alignment:** Share your strategic impact plan with your team. Involve them in setting goals and planning projects so that everyone is moving in the same direction. Collaborative planning fosters a shared commitment to long-term success.
- **Regular Strategic Reviews:** Hold periodic strategic review sessions with your team to assess progress, realign priorities, and celebrate successes. These reviews help maintain momentum and adapt to changes proactively.

- **Focus on Learning:** Cultivate a culture where learning from both successes and setbacks is valued. Encourage feedback and open dialogue about what strategies are working and where adjustments are needed.

The Lasting Benefits of a Well-Executed Impact Plan

When daily actions are purposefully aligned with long-term objectives, the cumulative impact can be extraordinary. Over time, this alignment leads to sustained growth, increased innovation, and the ability to weather challenges with confidence. A strategic impact plan transforms your vision from an abstract idea into a living, breathing process that drives meaningful change.

By ensuring that every step you take is deliberate and connected to your larger mission, you set yourself—and those around you—up for long-term success. The process of planning for impact is continuous and iterative; it demands regular reflection, adjustment, and a commitment to excellence in execution. Yet, the rewards are substantial: a sense of clarity, enhanced productivity, and a legacy defined by consistent, intentional progress.

Conclusion

Crafting vision and strategy is about more than just setting goals—it's about creating a coherent, inspiring, and actionable roadmap that connects your deepest values with your daily actions. In this chapter, we explored how to create a personal mission that serves as the foundation of your leadership, how to set strategic goals that are both measurable and achievable, and how to plan for impact by ensuring that every day's actions contribute to your long-term vision.

By defining your mission, you establish a clear purpose that guides every decision and action, even in the face of adversity. Strategic goal setting transforms your vision into specific, measurable targets, providing clarity and direction for your journey. Finally, planning for impact ensures that each day, each task, and each interaction is aligned with your overarching objectives, leading to sustained, meaningful change.

As you move forward, remember that vision and strategy are dynamic—continually evolving as you learn, grow, and adapt to new challenges and opportunities. Embrace the iterative nature of this process. Revisit your mission statement, refine your goals, and adjust your impact plan regularly to stay aligned with your aspirations and the realities of your environment.

A well-crafted vision and a strategic roadmap are the twin engines that drive impactful leadership. They empower you to transform challenges into opportunities, setbacks into stepping stones, and daily actions into the building blocks of a lasting legacy. By integrating the insights and practices from this chapter into your leadership style, you position yourself to not only achieve success but to inspire others to reach their full potential.

Every decision you make, every goal you set, and every plan you execute is a step on the journey toward a future defined by purpose and impact. Let your personal mission be your compass, your strategic goals your milestones, and your daily actions the tangible expressions of your vision. In doing so, you will craft a legacy that resonates with authenticity, drives innovation, and leaves a positive imprint on the world.

As you reflect on the insights shared in this chapter, consider the power of aligning your inner vision with your outer actions. Whether you are embarking on a new project, leading a team, or simply striving to be the best version of yourself, remember that every great achievement begins with a clear mission and a strategic plan. Commit to this process, and you will not only witness the transformation in your own life but also become a catalyst for change in the lives of those you lead.

Embrace the journey of crafting vision and strategy with passion and perseverance. Let your personal mission ignite your actions, your strategic goals guide your steps, and your plan for impact shape the future you wish to create. With clarity, commitment, and a relentless drive for excellence, you can transform your aspirations into achievements and build a leadership legacy that stands the test of time.

By integrating a powerful personal mission, robust strategic goal setting, and a daily plan for impact, you equip yourself with the essential tools to navigate the complexities of modern leadership. This chapter is your guide to turning abstract dreams into concrete outcomes—one thoughtful, purposeful action at a time. As you move forward with these strategies in hand, may you lead with vision, drive with strategy, and make an impact that endures.

Chapter 4: Leading with Influence

Influence is the currency of leadership. It is less about formal authority and more about the ability to inspire, persuade, and guide others toward a shared vision. In this chapter, we explore the art and science of leading with influence by focusing on three critical areas: mastering communication, inspiring others, and navigating conflict. Through real-world examples, practical exercises, and thoughtful analysis, you will learn how to harness the power of influence to build trust, motivate teams, and create a harmonious environment that drives progress.

Section 1: Mastering Communication

Effective communication is the cornerstone of influential leadership. It goes beyond simply conveying information—it involves inspiring confidence, fostering trust, and creating connections that resonate on both an emotional and intellectual level. Leaders who master communication can articulate complex ideas clearly, listen actively, and adapt their style to connect with diverse audiences.

The Role of Communication in Leadership

Communication is not just about speaking clearly; it's about creating a dialogue that invites participation, collaboration, and mutual understanding. As a leader, your words have the power to shape perceptions, build relationships, and ultimately, steer the direction of your team or organization. Consider these essential dimensions of communication:

- **Clarity and Precision:** When you communicate your ideas, clarity is key. Whether you are outlining a strategic vision or giving feedback, your message should be unambiguous and direct. This minimizes misunderstandings and ensures that everyone is on the same page.
- **Emotional Resonance:** Influential leaders are adept at connecting on an emotional level. Sharing personal stories, acknowledging challenges, and expressing genuine enthusiasm can transform routine messages into powerful calls to action.
- **Active Listening:** Communication is a two-way street. Effective leaders not only speak well but also listen intently. Active listening involves fully engaging with the speaker, validating their perspective, and responding thoughtfully.
- **Adaptability:** Different situations and audiences require different communication styles. Whether addressing a board of directors, a team of employees, or a community group, tailoring your language and tone to the context is crucial for impactful dialogue.

Strategies for Enhancing Communication Skills

1. **Develop a Clear Message:**

Before you speak, take a moment to clarify your purpose. What is the key idea you want to convey? Structure your message with a clear beginning, middle, and end. This practice ensures that your communication is purposeful and goal-oriented.

2. **Embrace Storytelling:**

Stories have the unique power to captivate and motivate. Use narratives that illustrate your values and vision. Whether it's an anecdote from your personal journey or a success story from your organization, storytelling creates an emotional connection that facts and figures alone cannot achieve.

3. **Practice Active Listening:**

Cultivate the habit of giving others your full attention. This means eliminating distractions, maintaining eye contact, and using verbal and non-verbal cues to show engagement. Ask clarifying questions to ensure you understand the speaker's perspective, and paraphrase their points to confirm understanding.

4. **Solicit Feedback:**

Regularly ask for feedback on your communication style. This could be through formal channels like surveys or informal discussions with peers and mentors. Constructive feedback helps you identify areas for improvement and reinforces your commitment to ongoing development.

5. **Utilize Non-Verbal Communication:**

Remember that communication isn't only verbal. Your body language, facial expressions, and tone of voice are powerful tools that complement your words. Strive for congruence between your verbal message and non-verbal signals to build trust and authenticity.

Exercises to Master Communication

- **Role-Playing:**

Simulate challenging conversations with a trusted colleague or mentor. Practice delivering difficult messages, handling objections, and navigating emotional responses. This exercise can boost your confidence and reveal areas for improvement.

- **Public Speaking Workshops:**

Join groups like Toastmasters or engage in public speaking courses. Regular practice in a supportive environment can help you refine your presentation skills, improve clarity, and learn to manage stage presence.

- **Reflective Journaling:**

After meetings or presentations, take time to write down what went well and what could be improved. Over time, patterns will emerge that can guide you in honing your communication skills.

- **Mindfulness Meditation:**

Incorporate mindfulness practices to enhance your focus and emotional regulation. A clear, present mind is better equipped to listen deeply and communicate effectively, even under pressure.

Overcoming Communication Barriers

Barriers to effective communication can come in many forms—cultural differences, personal biases, or simply the fast pace of modern life. To overcome these challenges, consider the following strategies:

- **Clarify Expectations:**

At the outset of any interaction, establish clear expectations for communication. This might involve setting agendas for meetings or outlining preferred methods of feedback.

- **Emphasize Empathy:**

Approach every conversation with empathy. Try to understand the feelings and perspectives of others, which can help bridge gaps in understanding and reduce conflict.

- **Simplify Complex Ideas:**

Break down complex concepts into manageable parts. Use analogies or visual aids to make abstract ideas more concrete. This is particularly useful when communicating with a diverse audience with varying levels of expertise.

- **Stay Present:**

Avoid multitasking during conversations. Focusing fully on the interaction not only improves comprehension but also demonstrates respect for the speaker.

The Impact of Mastering Communication

Leaders who excel in communication can transform team dynamics and foster a culture of openness and collaboration. By consistently delivering clear, compelling messages and actively engaging with your audience, you build a foundation of trust and credibility. This, in turn, enables you to inspire action, manage change, and lead your team with confidence.

Effective communication also serves as a preventive measure against misunderstandings and conflicts. When everyone is aligned through transparent dialogue, the likelihood of misinterpretation diminishes, paving the way for smoother operations and more harmonious relationships.

Section 2: Inspiring Others

True leadership is measured by your ability to inspire and elevate those around you. Inspiring others goes beyond motivating employees to meet targets—it involves igniting passion, fostering creativity, and building a shared sense of purpose within your community. When you inspire others, you create a ripple effect that transforms individuals into a cohesive force capable of achieving extraordinary outcomes.

The Art of Inspiration

Inspiration is both an art and a science. It begins with a deep understanding of what drives human behavior and what connects people to a larger purpose. As a leader, your role is to create an environment where every team member feels valued, capable, and motivated to contribute their best work.

- **Leading by Example:**

Your actions speak louder than words. When you embody the values and behaviors you wish to see in others, you set a powerful precedent. Authenticity, hard work, and resilience become contagious qualities that inspire your team.

- **Empowering Others:**

Provide your team with the autonomy to innovate and make decisions. Empowerment builds confidence and fosters a sense of ownership. When people feel trusted, they are more likely to take initiative and strive for excellence.

- **Sharing a Vision:**

Communicate a clear, compelling vision that resonates with your team's aspirations. A shared vision acts as a unifying force, aligning individual efforts with a collective goal. When everyone understands how their contributions fit into the bigger picture, motivation naturally follows.

- **Celebrating Successes:**

Recognize and celebrate both individual and team achievements. Public acknowledgment of success boosts morale and reinforces the behaviors you want to cultivate. Celebrations, whether big or small, help maintain a positive atmosphere and encourage ongoing commitment.

Techniques for Motivating Teams

1. Personalized Motivation:

Understand that each person is motivated by different factors. While some thrive on public recognition, others may prefer private acknowledgment or opportunities for professional development. Tailor your approach to meet the unique needs of each team member.

2. Setting Meaningful Challenges:

Encourage growth by setting challenging yet attainable goals. When people are pushed outside their comfort zones, they often discover hidden strengths and develop new skills. Ensure that these challenges are aligned with your overall vision so that the effort feels purposeful.

3. Creating a Culture of Trust:

Trust is the bedrock of inspiration. When your team trusts your leadership and believes in your vision, they are more willing to invest their energy and creativity. Transparency, consistent communication, and genuine care for your team's well-being are essential components of building trust.

4. Mentorship and Development:

Actively mentor and support the growth of your team members. Provide opportunities for learning, skill development, and career advancement. When people see that you are invested in their personal and professional growth, they are more likely to be inspired and committed.

5. **Encouraging Innovation:**

Foster an environment where new ideas are welcomed and explored. Encourage brainstorming sessions, cross-functional collaboration, and creative problem-solving. A culture that values innovation not only drives progress but also keeps team members engaged and inspired.

Exercises for Inspiring Others

- **Vision Workshops:**

Organize workshops where team members collaborate to refine and personalize the organizational vision. This collective exercise not only creates alignment but also deepens individual commitment to the shared goal.

- **Peer Recognition Programs:**

Implement a system where team members can recognize and reward each other's contributions. Peer recognition enhances morale and creates a supportive network within the team.

- **One-on-One Check-Ins:**

Schedule regular one-on-one meetings with team members to understand their aspirations, challenges, and feedback. These sessions provide a platform for personalized guidance and help build strong, trusting relationships.

- **Success Stories:**

Share stories of overcoming obstacles and achieving milestones, either from within your organization or from the broader community. These narratives can serve as powerful reminders that challenges can be transformed into opportunities for success.

The Transformative Power of Inspiration

When you inspire others, you create a momentum that can transform an entire organization. Inspiration leads to higher levels of engagement, creativity, and productivity. Team members who feel inspired are more resilient in the face of setbacks, more innovative in their problem-solving, and more committed to the overall mission.

Furthermore, an inspiring leader fosters a positive community culture. This influence extends beyond the workplace into personal lives and the wider community. By cultivating an environment of empowerment, trust, and shared purpose, you not only drive organizational success but also contribute to the development of future leaders who, in turn, will inspire others.

Section 3: Navigating Conflict

Conflict is inevitable in any dynamic organization or community. While it can be challenging, conflict also presents opportunities for growth, innovation, and deeper understanding. As a leader, your ability to navigate conflict effectively is a critical component of influencing those around you and maintaining a harmonious, progressive environment.

Understanding the Nature of Conflict

Conflicts often arise from differences in opinions, values, or goals. When managed properly, they can lead to constructive change and improved relationships. Recognizing that conflict is not inherently negative is the first step toward harnessing its potential. Instead of viewing conflict as a setback, see it as a catalyst for problem-solving and growth.

- **Types of Conflict:**

Conflict can manifest in many forms—from interpersonal disagreements to larger organizational disputes. It may stem from miscommunication, competition for resources, or differing expectations. Understanding the root cause of a conflict is essential for developing an effective resolution strategy.

- **The Role of Emotions:**

Emotions play a significant role in conflict situations. Frustration, anger, or fear can cloud judgment and escalate tensions. Leaders who can remain calm, objective, and empathetic are better equipped to mediate disputes and guide their teams toward resolution.

Strategies for Effective Conflict Resolution

1. **Active Mediation:**

As a leader, take an active role in mediating conflicts before they escalate. Facilitate open discussions where all parties have the opportunity to voice their perspectives. Act as a neutral moderator who guides the conversation toward common ground.

2. Empathetic Listening:

Listening with empathy means fully understanding the concerns and emotions of everyone involved. Encourage individuals to express their feelings and validate their experiences without immediately offering solutions. This approach builds trust and opens the door to collaborative problem-solving.

3. Establishing Ground Rules:

During conflict resolution sessions, establish clear ground rules that promote respectful dialogue. This might include guidelines such as no interrupting, avoiding blame, and focusing on the issues rather than personal attacks.

4. Focusing on Interests, Not Positions:

Encourage parties to discuss their underlying interests rather than rigid positions. By identifying common interests and shared goals, you can shift the conversation from confrontation to collaboration. This technique, often used in negotiation strategies, helps create win-win scenarios.

5. Leveraging Negotiation Techniques:

Equip yourself with negotiation strategies that are proven to work in high-stakes situations. Techniques such as principled negotiation—where you focus on objective criteria and mutually beneficial outcomes—can help in reaching agreements that satisfy all parties involved.

Practical Tools for Navigating Conflict

- **Conflict Mapping:**

Create a visual map of the conflict, outlining the key stakeholders, their positions, and underlying interests. This tool can help clarify the sources of tension and reveal areas where compromise is possible.

- **Role Reversal Exercises:**

Encourage conflicting parties to view the situation from the other's perspective. This exercise fosters empathy and often uncovers common ground that may not have been apparent initially.

- **Structured Dialogue Sessions:**

Organize sessions dedicated solely to conflict resolution. Use structured formats such as "talking circles" where each participant has a defined time to speak without interruption. This controlled environment can help reduce emotions and focus on problem-solving.

Handling Common Conflict Scenarios

- **Interpersonal Conflicts:**

When personal disagreements arise, encourage private, one-on-one discussions where individuals can express their concerns without an audience. As a leader, provide guidance on how to articulate issues constructively and work toward mutual understanding.

- **Team Disagreements:**

In cases where a whole team is affected by a conflict, facilitate group discussions that allow for collective problem-solving. Use brainstorming sessions to generate ideas for resolution and involve everyone in deciding on the best course of action.

- **Organizational Disputes:**

Larger conflicts may require formal conflict resolution mechanisms such as mediation or arbitration. Establish clear protocols for addressing these issues within your organization to ensure that conflicts are resolved fairly and transparently.

Maintaining Harmony While Driving Progress

Conflict resolution is not just about quelling disputes—it's about transforming conflict into a constructive force. By addressing conflicts head-on, you can prevent resentment, maintain team cohesion, and even spark innovation. A well-handled conflict can lead to new ideas, improved processes, and a stronger, more unified team.

- **Creating a Safe Environment:**

Foster an environment where team members feel safe to express dissenting opinions. When people know that their perspectives are valued, conflicts can be addressed openly and resolved before they escalate.

- **Balancing Firmness and Flexibility:**

As a leader, you must strike a balance between being firm in upholding values and being flexible enough to consider alternative solutions. This balance ensures that conflicts are resolved without compromising the core principles of your organization.

- **Post-Conflict Reflection:**

After a conflict is resolved, take time to reflect on the process. What lessons were learned? How can future conflicts be managed more effectively? This reflection not only improves conflict resolution skills but also strengthens the overall resilience of the team.

Exercises for Conflict Navigation

- **Simulation Drills:**

Organize simulation drills that mimic common conflict scenarios. Role-playing these situations in a controlled environment can help you and your team develop effective strategies for real-life disputes.

- **Feedback Forums:**

Create regular forums for team members to provide feedback on interpersonal dynamics and potential areas of friction. Early identification of issues can prevent conflicts from escalating and promote a culture of continuous improvement.

- **Conflict Resolution Workshops:**

Invest in professional development workshops focused on conflict resolution and negotiation. These sessions provide both theoretical frameworks and practical techniques that can be applied immediately in your organization.

The Long-Term Benefits of Navigating Conflict Effectively

Leaders who master conflict resolution not only maintain harmony but also drive progress. By converting conflicts into opportunities for dialogue and innovation, you build a resilient organization that can adapt to challenges and emerge stronger. The ability to navigate conflict effectively enhances your influence and reinforces your reputation as a leader who can steer the team through adversity.

Conclusion

Leading with influence is a multifaceted endeavor that demands mastery over communication, a genuine ability to inspire others, and the skill to navigate conflict constructively. In this chapter, we examined how to harness the power of communication to build trust and convey a clear, compelling message; how to inspire and empower others by sharing a resonant vision and fostering a culture of innovation and trust; and how to approach conflict not as a stumbling block, but as an opportunity for growth and transformation.

By mastering communication, you lay the groundwork for every other aspect of influence. When your words resonate with clarity and emotion, you create connections that inspire action and loyalty. When you inspire others, you ignite a passion that transforms ordinary teams into dynamic communities driven by shared purpose. And when you navigate conflict with empathy and strategic insight, you turn challenges into stepping stones for progress, fostering an environment where every voice is heard and every challenge is an opportunity.

The journey to leading with influence is continuous. It requires reflection, practice, and an unwavering commitment to personal and organizational growth. As you implement the strategies, exercises, and techniques outlined in this chapter, remember that influence is not about power—it's about service, integrity, and the relentless pursuit of excellence. Every conversation you initiate, every team you empower, and every conflict you resolve contributes to a legacy of leadership that leaves a lasting, positive impact on the world.

Embrace the challenge of leading with influence with passion and perseverance. Strive to communicate with clarity and compassion, inspire others by aligning their aspirations with a greater purpose, and transform conflicts into opportunities for meaningful change. In doing so, you not only enhance your leadership skills but also set in motion a ripple effect that will elevate your team, your organization, and your community.

May you continue to refine your influence, knowing that every effort you make today builds the foundation for a more connected, inspired, and resilient tomorrow.

By integrating these principles into your leadership practice, you empower yourself to lead with a presence that not only commands respect but also cultivates trust, motivation, and lasting impact. Whether you are guiding a small team or steering an entire organization, the influence you wield comes from your commitment to clear communication, the inspiration you instill in others, and your ability to navigate and transform conflict into a pathway for progress.

As you move forward, let these strategies serve as a roadmap. Reflect on your interactions, seek feedback, and continuously adapt your approach. Remember that leadership is a journey—one that is measured not just by the results you achieve, but by the positive influence you have on the lives of those around you.

Embrace the art of influence, and become the leader who inspires, connects, and creates meaningful change in every sphere of your life.

Chapter 5: Sustaining Legacy and Growth

In leadership, success is not solely defined by immediate achievements but by the enduring impact you create and the continuous evolution of your abilities. Chapter 5 explores how to sustain your legacy and growth as a leader. In this chapter, you will learn how to commit to lifelong growth through reflection, feedback, and ongoing education; how to maintain a long-term focus even in the midst of daily challenges; and how to craft a legacy that ensures your leadership leaves a meaningful, enduring mark. This chapter provides a detailed roadmap to help you remain adaptable, aligned with your personal mission, and primed for making lasting contributions in your community and beyond.

Section 1: Embracing Continuous Learning

The Imperative of Lifelong Learning

In today's ever-changing world, the journey of leadership is one of constant evolution. Embracing continuous learning is not simply about acquiring new knowledge or skills; it is a mindset—a commitment to perpetual growth that keeps you adaptable and innovative. Continuous learning allows you to remain relevant, to refine your leadership practices, and to set an example for those who follow in your footsteps.

Lifelong learning is rooted in the belief that every experience, challenge, and success offers an opportunity to learn. Whether it's through formal education, self-directed study, or experiential learning, the process of continuously expanding your knowledge base is a key ingredient to long-term leadership success.

Strategies for Continuous Learning

1. **Regular Reflection:**
2. Set aside dedicated time each week or month for reflection. Consider what went well in your recent endeavors, what could be improved, and how these insights align with your long-term vision. Journaling your experiences is a

powerful tool in capturing lessons learned and mapping out areas for future growth.

3. Seeking Feedback:

Feedback is one of the most potent catalysts for growth. Create a culture of open dialogue within your team or network. Encourage colleagues, mentors, and even those you lead to provide constructive feedback on your performance. This feedback can reveal blind spots, validate your strengths, and guide your developmental focus.

4. Formal and Informal Education:

Enroll in workshops, courses, or certificate programs that enhance your leadership competencies. At the same time, don't underestimate the value of informal education—reading books, listening to podcasts, and attending seminars can provide fresh perspectives and spark innovative ideas.

5. Mentorship and Peer Learning:

Engage with mentors who have traversed paths similar to your own. Likewise, participate in peer groups where leaders share experiences and insights. These relationships can offer both practical advice and emotional support as you navigate complex challenges.

6. Embracing New Technologies:

With rapid technological advancements, staying abreast of new tools and platforms can be instrumental in keeping your skills relevant. Learn how emerging technologies can enhance your strategic planning, team collaboration, and even your communication with stakeholders.

Exercises and Practices for Continuous Learning

- **Reflection Journals:**

Keep a detailed journal of your daily experiences. Write about the challenges you encountered, decisions you made, and the outcomes of those decisions. Over time, review your entries to identify recurring themes or lessons that could inform your future actions.

- **360-Degree Feedback Surveys:**

Implement periodic 360-degree feedback surveys where peers, subordinates, and supervisors can evaluate your leadership style. Use this data to create a personalized development plan that addresses both strengths and areas for improvement.

- **Learning Goals:**

Establish specific learning goals with measurable outcomes. For example, you might set a goal to read one leadership book per month, attend a quarterly webinar, or master a new project management tool within six months. Tracking these goals ensures that learning remains an intentional part of your routine.

- **Book Clubs or Discussion Groups:**

Organize or join a book club focused on leadership and personal development topics. Group discussions can provide diverse insights and foster a deeper understanding of new ideas.

The Role of Curiosity and Humility

Two qualities are central to embracing continuous learning: curiosity and humility. Curiosity propels you to ask questions, seek new experiences, and venture into uncharted territories. It is the drive that encourages exploration beyond the familiar. Humility, on the other hand, allows you to recognize that there is always more to learn. Even as an accomplished leader, acknowledging that you don't have all the answers opens the door to new insights and continuous improvement.

Learning from Failure and Success

Every experience, whether a triumph or a setback, is a rich source of learning. Reflect on both your successes and failures, and analyze them with an objective mindset. Ask yourself:

- What did I do that led to this success?
- Which strategies contributed to my failure?
- How can I replicate my successes and avoid past mistakes in the future?

By viewing failures as learning opportunities, you foster resilience and enhance your problem-solving skills. This iterative learning process helps you fine-tune your leadership approach over time.

The Benefits of a Continuous Learning Mindset

Adopting a continuous learning mindset yields several long-term benefits:

- **Increased Adaptability:**

By continually updating your knowledge and skills, you become more adaptable to changes in your industry, technology, and the broader economic landscape.

- **Enhanced Creativity and Innovation:**

Exposure to diverse perspectives and new ideas fuels creativity. A leader who values learning is better positioned to innovate and lead transformational change.

- **Stronger Team Engagement:**

When you commit to learning, you model that behavior for your team. This can create a culture where continuous improvement is celebrated and where everyone is motivated to grow.

- **Personal Fulfillment:**

The pursuit of knowledge and growth enriches your personal and professional life, leading to a deeper sense of fulfillment and purpose.

Section 2: Maintaining Long-Term Focus

The Challenge of Long-Term Vision in a Fast-Paced World

In a world of constant change and immediate demands, maintaining a long-term focus can be a formidable challenge. Daily urgencies, shifting market trends, and the distractions of modern life can easily divert your attention from your broader mission. Yet, sustaining long-term focus is essential for achieving lasting impact and ensuring that your leadership remains grounded in your core purpose.

Strategies for Long-Term Focus

1. **Establish a Clear Vision and Mission:**

Your long-term focus starts with a well-defined vision and mission. Revisit your personal mission statement regularly to ensure it remains aligned with your evolving goals. This statement should serve as a north star, guiding your decisions and actions over time.

2. Set Milestones and Benchmarks:

Break down your long-term objectives into smaller, manageable milestones. Establish clear benchmarks that mark your progress along the way. These milestones help maintain momentum and provide opportunities to celebrate progress, reinforcing your commitment to the overall vision.

3. Develop Daily Routines that Support Long-Term Goals:

Create habits and routines that keep you aligned with your long-term objectives. Whether it's a morning meditation session, a daily review of your goals, or a regular planning session at the end of the day, these practices help you stay focused and intentional.

4. Prioritize and Delegate:

Focus on activities that directly contribute to your long-term vision, and delegate tasks that do not require your direct involvement. Effective delegation not only frees up your time for strategic planning but also empowers your team to take on greater responsibility.

5. Use Visualization Techniques:

Visualization is a powerful tool for maintaining long-term focus. Create vision boards, write detailed future scenarios, or use guided imagery exercises to keep your end goals vividly in mind. These techniques can boost your motivation and remind you of the impact you aim to achieve.

Overcoming Short-Term Distractions

Short-term distractions are inevitable, but with the right strategies, you can minimize their impact:

- **Time Blocking:**

Allocate specific time slots for focused work on long-term projects. Protect these blocks from interruptions by setting boundaries and communicating your availability clearly.

- **Digital Detoxes:**

Periodically disconnect from digital distractions such as social media, emails, or non-essential notifications. This helps you maintain clarity and prevents the overload that can derail long-term planning.

- **Mindfulness Practices:**

Regular mindfulness or meditation sessions can improve your concentration and reduce stress. These practices help you stay present and focused on your priorities, even when faced with short-term challenges.

Aligning Actions with Vision

Consistency is key to maintaining long-term focus. Every action you take should be a deliberate step toward your larger vision. To achieve this alignment:

- **Review Your Calendar:**

Start each day by reviewing your schedule and asking, "How do these activities move me closer to my long-term goals?" If an activity does not serve your vision, consider postponing it or delegating it.

- **Regular Strategic Reviews:**

Conduct quarterly or annual strategic reviews of your progress. Reflect on your accomplishments, reassess your priorities, and adjust your plans as needed. This structured reflection helps ensure that you remain on track over time.

- **Balance Urgency with Importance:**

Learn to differentiate between tasks that are urgent and those that are important. While urgent tasks demand immediate attention, important tasks are the ones that drive long-term success. Prioritize the latter to avoid getting caught up in day-to-day crises.

The Importance of Resilience and Adaptability

Maintaining a long-term focus requires resilience and the ability to adapt. As circumstances change, your strategy may need to evolve. Embrace change as part of the process rather than viewing it as a disruption. Flexibility in your approach ensures that you can navigate unforeseen challenges without losing sight of your ultimate objectives.

Exercises for Sustaining Long-Term Focus

- **Long-Term Goal Mapping:**

Create a detailed map of your long-term objectives, including the milestones you need to reach along the way. Visual representations of your goals can serve as constant reminders of your path forward.

- **Daily Reflection Rituals:**

At the end of each day, spend a few minutes reflecting on what you accomplished and how those actions aligned with your long-term goals. This ritual can help you identify patterns and adjust your approach as necessary.

- **Accountability Partnerships:**

Pair up with a peer or mentor who shares similar long-term aspirations. Regular check-ins with your accountability partner can help you stay committed, provide support during setbacks, and celebrate progress together.

The Long-Term Rewards

Maintaining a long-term focus not only helps you achieve your strategic goals but also creates a sustainable framework for growth. By continuously aligning your daily actions with your broader vision, you build momentum and foster a sense of purpose that can withstand the pressures of day-to-day operations. In the long run, this disciplined focus contributes to a legacy of thoughtful, impactful leadership.

Section 3: Crafting Your Legacy

Defining Legacy in Leadership

Crafting your legacy is about more than leaving behind a list of achievements; it's about creating a lasting impact that inspires future generations. A legacy is the cumulative result of your values, actions, and the influence you have on others. It embodies not only the successes you achieve but also the principles you uphold and the culture you foster within your organization and community.

Your legacy is built over time through consistent, intentional actions. It is the story you leave behind—a narrative of resilience, innovation, and a commitment to making the world a better place. Crafting your legacy requires you to think beyond short-term gains and focus on the enduring mark you wish to imprint on society.

Steps to Crafting a Meaningful Legacy

   1. Clarify Your Core Values:

Reflect deeply on the principles that define your leadership. These core values should be evident in every decision you make and every initiative you undertake. A clear understanding of your values provides a foundation for building a legacy that is authentic and impactful.

   2. Develop a Long-Term Impact Plan:

Outline specific actions and projects that will contribute to your legacy. Consider the areas where you want to make a difference—be it in community development, innovation, education, or corporate governance. Create a strategic plan that details the steps you will take, the resources you will invest, and the milestones you expect to achieve.

   3. Mentor Future Leaders:

One of the most powerful ways to leave a lasting legacy is to invest in the development of others. Actively mentor emerging leaders and create opportunities for them to grow. By nurturing talent, you ensure that your vision and values continue to influence future generations.

   4. Document and Share Your Journey:

Whether through writing, speaking engagements, or digital media, share your experiences, insights, and lessons learned. Documenting your journey not only preserves your legacy but also inspires others to pursue their own paths of excellence.

5. Create Sustainable Initiatives:

Develop programs or initiatives that are designed to endure beyond your direct involvement. Whether it's a scholarship fund, a community project, or an innovation lab, sustainable initiatives serve as living testaments to your commitment to long-term impact.

Strategies for Building a Leadership Brand

Your personal brand as a leader is an integral part of your legacy. A strong leadership brand is built on consistency, integrity, and a clear vision. Consider these strategies:

- **Consistent Messaging:**

Ensure that your public communications, actions, and decisions consistently reflect your values and mission. This consistency builds trust and makes your legacy recognizable.

- **Public Engagement:**

Engage with your community through speaking events, interviews, and social media. By sharing your insights and engaging with diverse audiences, you amplify your influence and inspire others.

- **Thought Leadership:**

Position yourself as an expert in your field by contributing to publications, participating in panel discussions, and hosting workshops. Thought leadership not only enhances your credibility but also cements your reputation as a visionary leader.

Overcoming Challenges in Legacy Building

Building a lasting legacy is not without challenges. Common obstacles include shifting market dynamics, internal resistance to change, and the pressures of short-term performance metrics. To overcome these challenges:

- **Stay True to Your Values:**

In times of uncertainty, return to your core values. These guiding principles will help you navigate challenges without compromising on your vision.

- **Be Patient and Persistent:**

A legacy is built over years, not months. Recognize that setbacks are part of the journey and maintain a long-term perspective even when progress seems slow.

- **Foster a Culture of Innovation:**

Encourage creativity and open dialogue within your team. A dynamic culture that welcomes new ideas is more likely to sustain your initiatives long after you have moved on.

Exercises for Crafting Your Legacy

- **Legacy Vision Statement:**

Write a detailed vision statement that outlines the impact you want to have in the next 10, 20, or 30 years. Include specific goals, the communities you wish to serve, and the values that will drive your actions. Revisit and refine this statement as your journey evolves.

- **Mentorship Circles:**

Establish a mentorship program or circle where you regularly engage with emerging leaders. Use these sessions to impart wisdom, discuss challenges, and co-create strategies for sustainable impact.

- **Impact Metrics:**

Develop a set of metrics that measure not just financial or operational success, but also social impact, cultural change, and innovation. Regularly review these metrics to assess the long-term effect of your initiatives.

The Emotional and Psychological Aspects of Legacy

Crafting a legacy is as much about emotional intelligence as it is about strategic planning. It involves understanding the stories and emotions of those you lead, and ensuring that your influence is felt not only in outcomes but also in the hearts of people. Cultivate empathy, celebrate human connections, and recognize that the true measure of your legacy is the positive impact you have on the lives of others.

The Enduring Benefits of a Well-Crafted Legacy

A lasting legacy benefits not only the leader but also the broader community. When your leadership leaves an enduring mark:

- **Future Leaders Are Inspired:**

Your values, stories, and initiatives serve as a blueprint for others, encouraging them to pursue excellence and integrity.

- **Cultural Transformation:**

The legacy of your leadership can shift organizational culture, setting higher standards for ethics, innovation, and community engagement.

- **Long-Term Impact:**

Sustainable initiatives, mentorship programs, and documented wisdom ensure that the impact of your leadership continues to grow and evolve, long after your direct involvement.

Integrating Legacy with Daily Leadership Practices

A legacy is built through daily actions that align with your long-term vision. Here are a few practices to help integrate legacy building into your routine:

- **Daily Reflection on Impact:**

Conclude each day by reflecting on how your actions contributed to your larger vision. Consider what you did to empower others, drive innovation, or uphold your values.

- **Celebrating Incremental Wins:**

Recognize and celebrate small victories that contribute to your long-term goals. These celebrations not only boost morale but also reinforce the behaviors that form your legacy.

- **Documentation and Storytelling:**

Regularly document your journey through blogs, articles, or videos. Storytelling is a powerful tool that immortalizes your experiences and shares your wisdom with a wider audience.

Conclusion

Sustaining legacy and growth is the culmination of a lifelong commitment to excellence, integrity, and continuous improvement. In this chapter, you have explored the vital practices that ensure your leadership journey is not only about achieving immediate successes but also about leaving a lasting impact. By embracing continuous learning, you commit to a dynamic process of self-improvement that keeps you at the forefront of innovation and personal development. Maintaining long-term focus ensures that, amid the chaos of daily life, your actions remain aligned with your core mission and vision. And by crafting your legacy, you set the stage for a future where your values, insights, and leadership style inspire generations to come.

As you integrate the strategies outlined in this chapter into your leadership practice, remember that legacy is built one deliberate action at a time. Whether it is through daily reflection, active mentorship, or the sustainable initiatives you launch, every step you take contributes to a broader narrative of impact and purpose. Your legacy is a testament to the power of aligning your personal mission with the needs of your community and the aspirations of future leaders.

Let this chapter serve as a reminder that leadership is not a destination but a journey—a continuous cycle of learning, focusing, and giving back. By dedicating yourself to lifelong growth, staying true to your long-term vision, and strategically crafting your legacy, you create an enduring foundation for success that transcends individual achievements.

Embrace the process with passion and perseverance, knowing that each lesson learned, each milestone reached, and each life touched adds another chapter to your leadership story. Your journey of sustaining legacy and growth is not only about the impact you create today but also about the inspiration and guidance you leave for tomorrow's leaders.

May you continue to learn, grow, and lead with the conviction that every step you take contributes to a brighter, more impactful future. In your pursuit of legacy, remain open to new ideas, stay grounded in your values, and always strive to leave the world a better place than you found it.

By integrating continuous learning, long-term focus, and legacy crafting into your daily leadership practice, you empower yourself to create a future defined by enduring impact. As you forge ahead on this journey, remember that the quality of your legacy is measured not only by what you achieve but by the lives you inspire, the values you uphold, and the lasting influence you impart on your community.

Embrace each day as an opportunity to reinforce your commitment to excellence. Reflect on your experiences, seek out opportunities for growth, and invest in the development of others. In doing so, you ensure that your leadership is not confined to the present but extends into the future, shaping a legacy that will inspire, empower, and transform lives for generations to come.

Your legacy is the sum of your actions, the wisdom you share, and the passion you infuse into every endeavor. Craft it with intention, lead with heart, and let your journey of sustaining legacy and growth be the foundation for a truly remarkable leadership story.

Made in the USA
Coppell, TX
28 March 2025

47652365R00050